BELLY LAUGHS

Jokes for Kids

Jokes for Kids

AMIR YAZ

Illustrated by Bobby Steele

This book is a work of fiction. The names, characters and events in this book are the products of the author's imagination or are used fictitiously. Any similarity to real persons living or dead is coincidental and not intended by the author.

Belly Laughs: Jokes for Kids

Copyright © 2022 by Amir Yaz
All rights reserved. Neither this book, nor any parts within it may be sold or reproduced in any form or by any electronic or mechanical means, including information storage and retrieval systems, without permission in writing from the author. The only exception is by a reviewer, who may quote short excerpts in a review.

Published by Belly Laughs
Belly Laughs Comedy Club LLC

bellylaughscomedy.com
Illustrations by Bobby Steele.

Belly Laughs: Jokes for Kids / Amir Yaz
ISBN (paperback): 9781736736401

Library of Congress Control Number: 2022950023

eISBN: 9781662935374

This book is dedicated to my nephew Leo, my little brother Aaron, and to my fellow Hydro Warriors who are living with hydrocephalus.

I had a novel idea...

so I decided to
write a book.

I went hiking and ran
into an 8-foot bear...

I have no idea how
it even walked with
that many feet.

My cat got her first job...

at the scratching post office.

Cats aren't very environmentally friendly.

They KITTY LITTER!

What do you call
a cow that tells
bad jokes?

CORNY BEEF!

**What do cows drink
in the morning?**

DE-CALF!

How does an evil cow laugh?

MOOHAHAHA!

How does a pig
defend itself?

With PORK CHOPS!

What did the buck say to the doe when she asked him if he took out the garbage?

YES DEER!

How does a bee
brush his hair?

With a HONEY COMB!

Where do gorilla's go to work out?

The JUNGLE GYM!

My dog...

is really into
flea markets.

A rabbit burger...

is ALWAYS fast food.

Did you hear
about the turkey
who ate too much?

He was STUFFED!

Did you hear about
the chef that was
also a comedian?

His food tasted funny.

My friend gave me
a bag of onions for
my birthday...

I was so touched; it
drove me to tears!

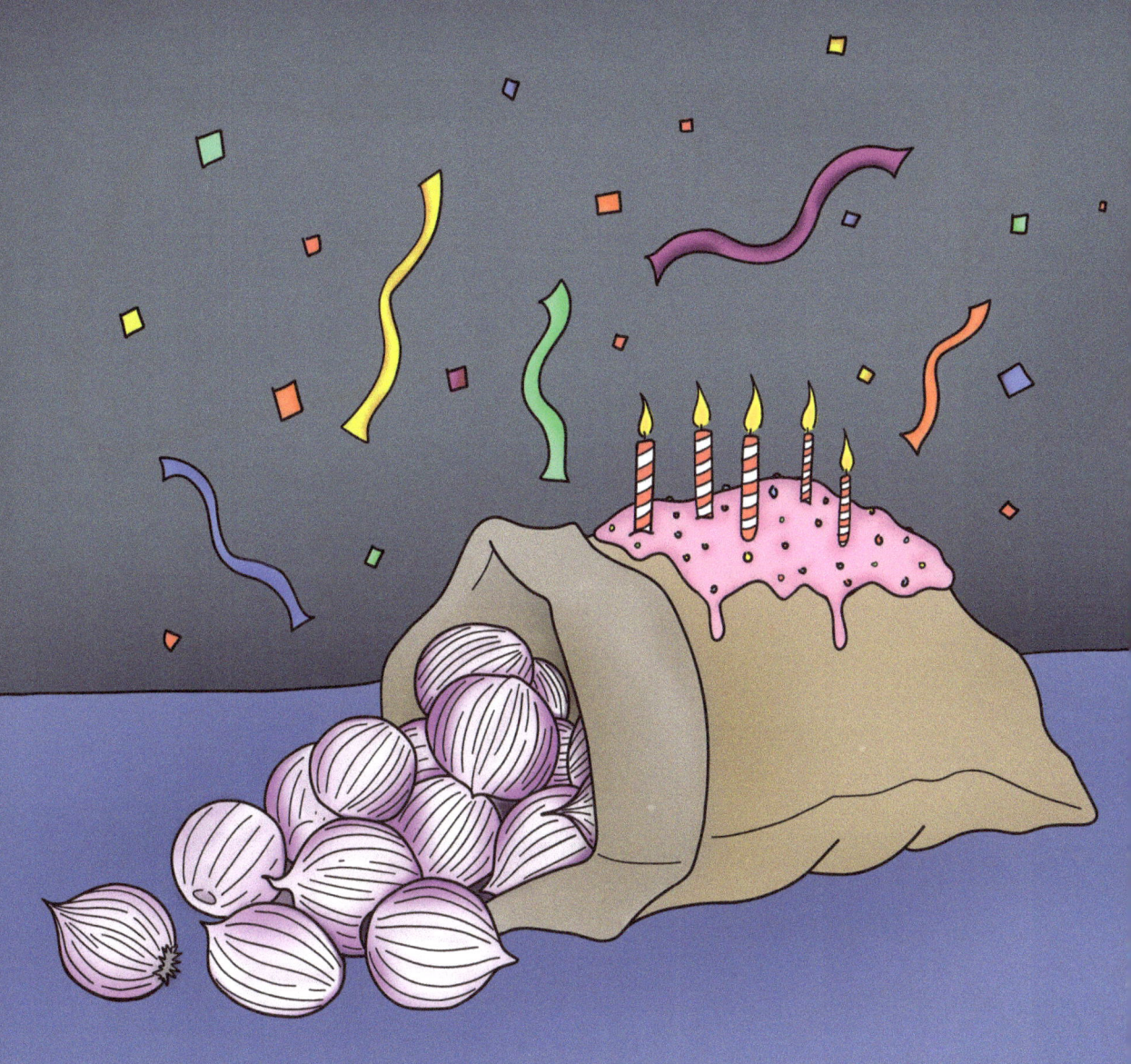

My belly button
just graduated...

from the
NAVEL ACADEMY!

Dr. Frankenstein...

was the first
BODY BUILDER!

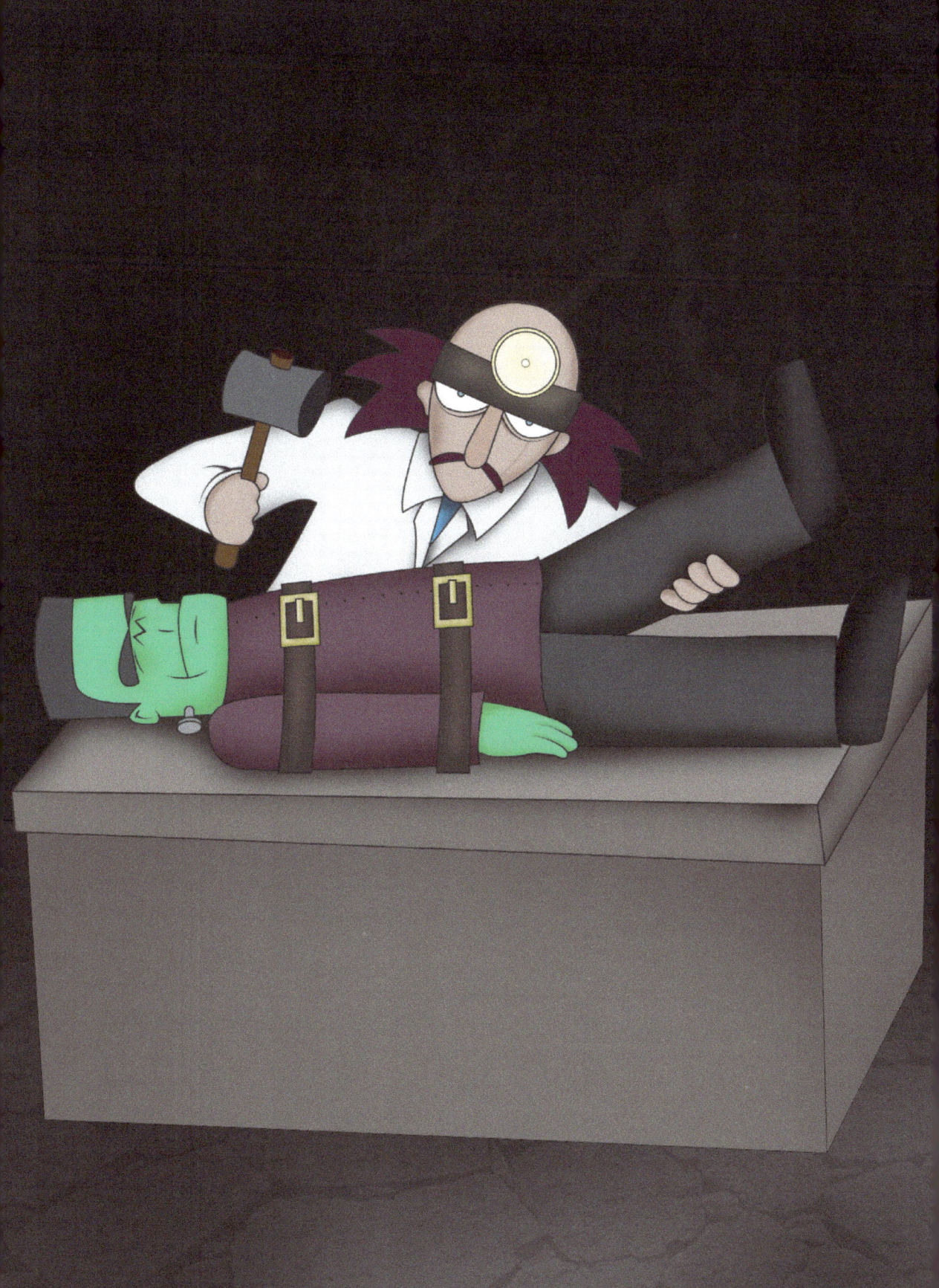

I wonder if wizards and witches...

use spell check.

I wanted to
go bowling...

so I brought my
SPARE shoes.

I wanted to go
boating, but it
was too expensive.

I was waiting
for a SAIL!

I bought a boat off
the internet.

It came with
FREE SHIPPING!

I always take
my dates boating...

because I'm
ROWmantic.

Why did the dragon go to his high school reunion?

To catch up with his old FLAME!

I wanted to go
to Gettysburg,
but I got lost.

I couldn't find
the address.

Did you hear about the book that got shot?

There was a hole in the story!!!

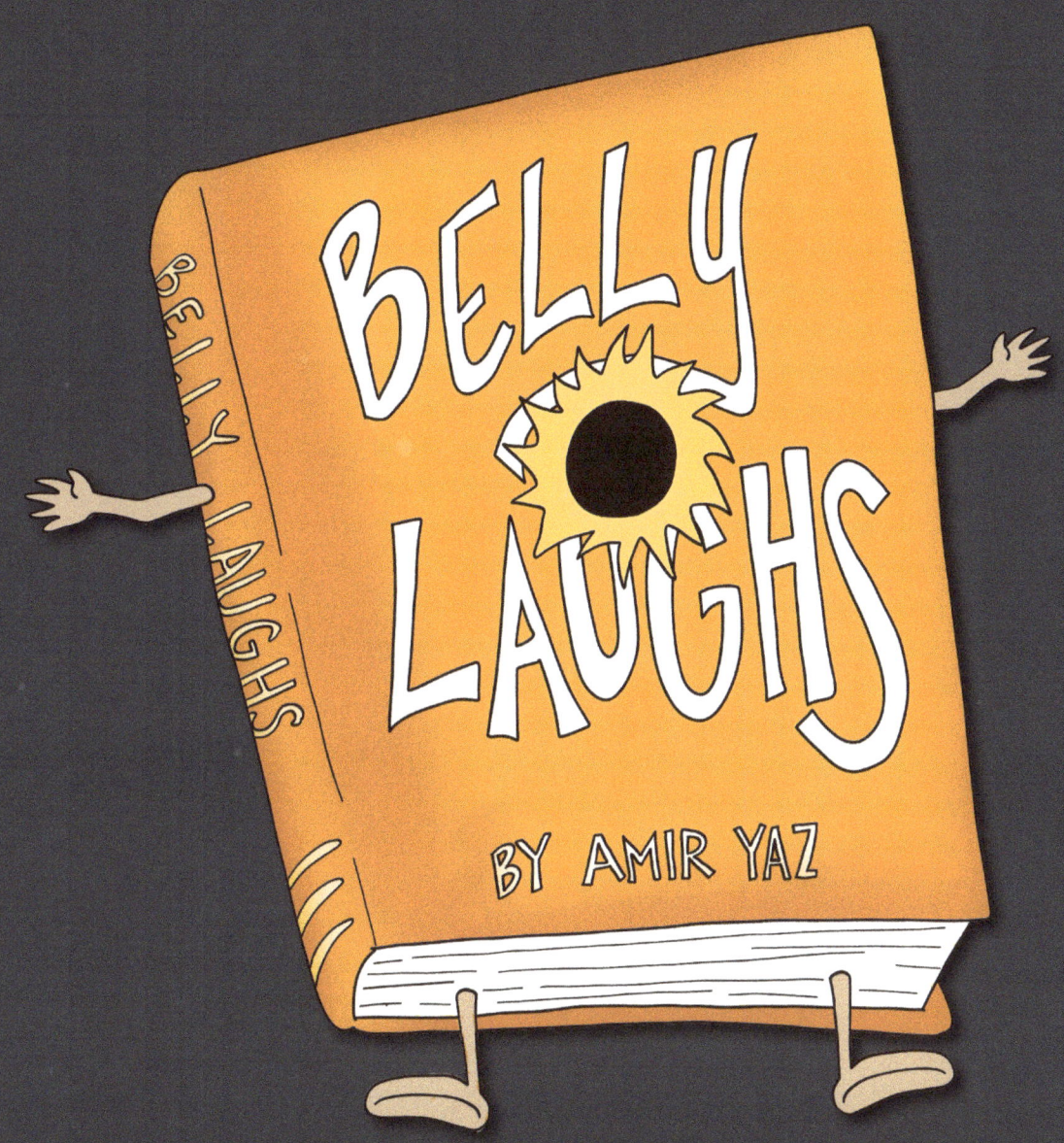

My left foot...

really wants to
go to TOE-kio!

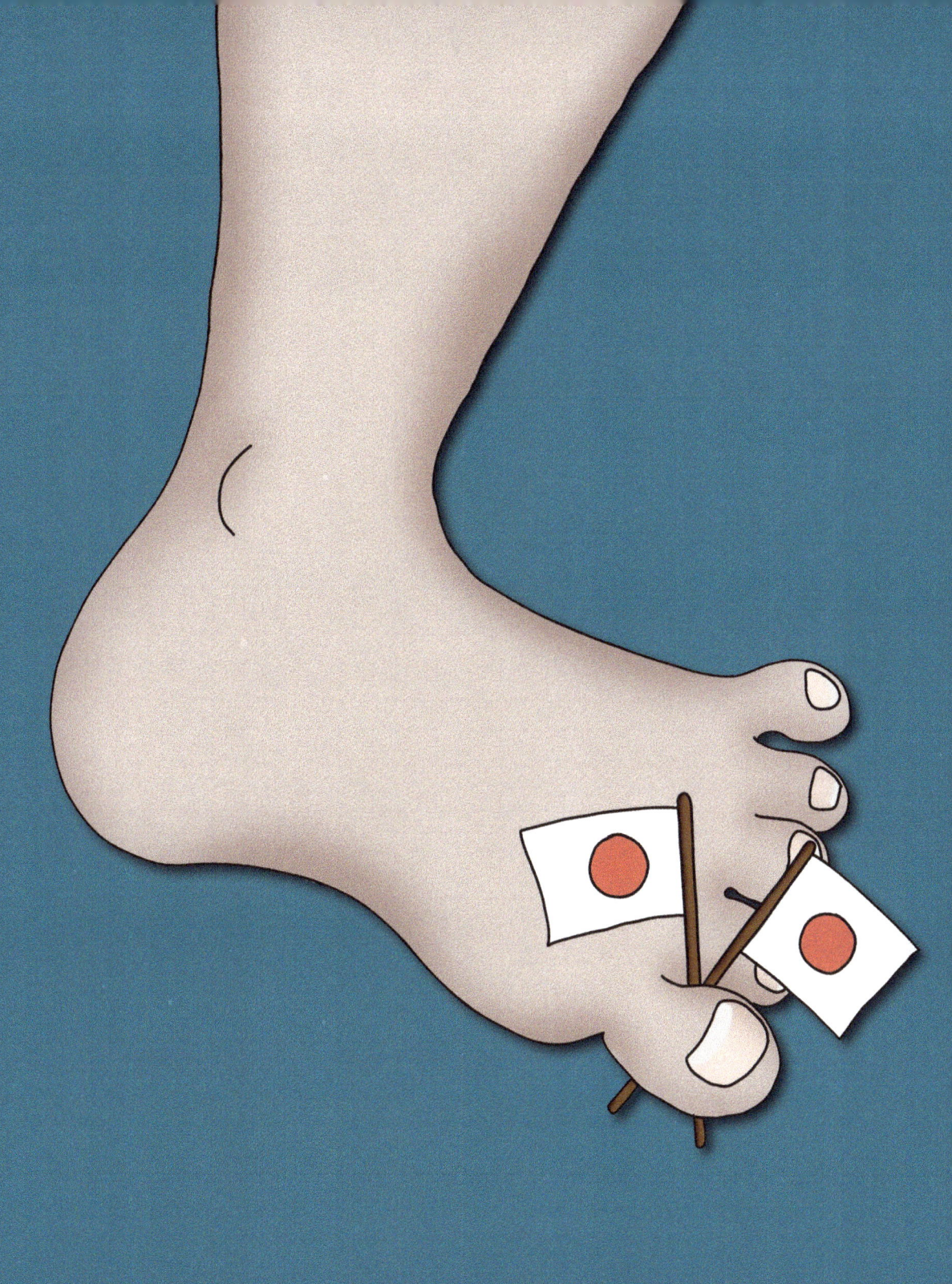

Time flies...

if you're a watch on a plane.

They have
good karaoke...

in SINGapore!

My air conditioning
broke today...

NOT COOL!

I fell for a
pyramid scheme...

IN EGYPT!

The first stationary bike...

was made out of paper.

About the author

Amir Yaz is a stand-up comedy producer, comedian, and now, first-time author. He has always loved reading joke books from a very young age and wanted to put smiles on kids' faces, so he created this illustrated children's joke book with the help of his friend Bobby Steele.

Amir was born with hydrocephalus. It is an accumulation of fluid in the brain that cannot drain naturally. It requires a shunt that aids in draining the fluid. The only treatment is brain surgery and there is no cure for the condition. A portion of the proceeds from each book sold will be donated to the Hydrocephalus Association.

www.ingramcontent.com/pod-product-compliance
Lightning Source LLC
Chambersburg PA
CBHW051318110526
44590CB00031B/4396